P9-CQV-733

LET'S LOOK AT
PERU

BY NIKKI BRUNO CLAPPER

CAPSTONE PRESS
a capstone imprint

Pebble Plus is published by Capstone Press,
1710 Roe Crest Drive, North Mankato, Minnesota 56003
www.mycapstone.com

Library of Congress Cataloging-in-Publication Data
Names: Clapper, Nikki Bruno, author.
Title: Let's look at Peru / by Nikki Bruno Clapper.
Description: North Mankato, Minnesota : Capstone Press, [2018] | Series:
  Pebble plus. Let's look at countries | Includes bibliographical references
  and index. | Audience: Ages 4-8.
Identifiers: LCCN 2017037876 (print) | LCCN 2017038079 (ebook) | ISBN
  9781515799276 (eBook PDF) | ISBN 9781515799153 (hardcover) | ISBN
  9781515799214 (pbk.)
Subjects: LCSH: Peru--Juvenile literature.
Classification: LCC F3408.5 (ebook) | LCC F3408.5 .B78 2018 (print) | DDC
  985--dc23
LC record available at https://lccn.loc.gov/2017037876

Editorial Credits
Juliette Peters, designer; Tracy Cummins, media researcher; Laura Manthe, production specialist

Photo Credits
Newscom: Michael & Patricia Fogden/Minden Pictures, 11; Shutterstock: Alfredo Cerra, 17,
Byelikova Oksana, 22-23, 24, Christian Vinces, Cover Top, Cover Middle, 1, 15, Foodio, 19, Fotos593,
5, Gabor Kovacs Photography, 13, Gil C, 22 top, Mikadun, 3, nale, 4, ostill, 14, Pavel Svoboda
Photography, 6-7, Pere Rubi, 9, Salparadis, Cover Bottom, Cover Back, spacaj, 21, Vadim Petrakov, 10

Note to Parents and Teachers

The Let's Look at Countries set supports national curriculum standards for social studies related
to people, places, and culture. This book describes and illustrates Peru. The images support early
readers in understanding the text. The repetition of words and phrases helps early readers learn
new words. This book also introduces early readers to subject-specific vocabulary words, which are
defined in the Glossary section. Early readers may need assistance to read some words and to use
the Table of Contents, Glossary, Read More, Internet Sites, Critical Thinking Questions, and Index
sections of the book.

Printed in the United States of America.
010774S18

TABLE OF CONTENTS

Where Is Peru?

Peru is a country in South America. It is about twice the size of the U.S. state of Texas. Peru's capital is Lima.

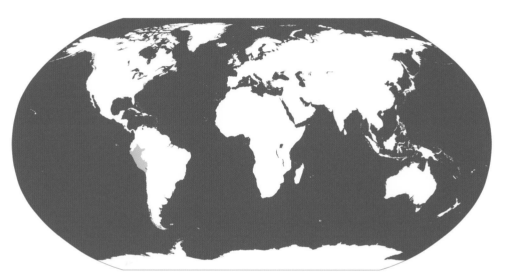

Peru

Three Regions

Peru has three regions from west to east. First is the coastal desert. Next are the Andes Mountains. Then comes the rain forest.

Andes Mountains

Peru's coast gets very little rain. The climate is cold in the Andes. But most of Peru is wet and hot. It is part of the Amazon Rain Forest.

Amazon Rain Forest

In the Wild

Penguins live on Peru's coast.

Llamas wander the mountains.

The rain forest is home to

jaguars and tapirs.

penguin

tapir

People

About half of Peru's people

are Quechua Indians.

Other people have come

to Peru from Europe and Asia.

Quechua Indians

On the Job

Some Peruvians farm or fish for a living. Others work in silver or copper mines. Jobs in tourism are growing.

Celebrations

Most Peruvians are Catholic.

Each town has a festival

for its special patron saint.

Corpus Christi is a big

holiday in June.

At the Table

Peruvians eat a lot
of seafood, grains, and
potatoes. Ceviche is a
popular dish. It has fish,
lime juice, and hot peppers.

ceviche

Famous Site

Machu Picchu is an old city
high in the Andes Mountains.
The Inca people built it
in about 1450. Machu Picchu
has amazing views!

QUICK PERU FACTS

Peru's flag

Name: Republic of Peru

Capital: Lima

Other major cities: Arequipa, Trujillo, Cuzco

Population: 30,741,062 (July 2016 estimate)

Size: 496,224 square miles (1,285,216 sq km)

Languages: Spanish, Quechua, Aymara

Money: nuevo sol

GLOSSARY

capital—the city in a country where the government is based

climate—average weather of a place throughout the year

patron saint—a saint who is believed to look after a particular country or group of people; a saint is a person honored by the Catholic church because of his or her very holy life

region—a large area

tourism—the business of taking care of visitors to a country or place

READ MORE

Franchino, Vicky. *Amazon Rain Forest.* Community Connections: Getting to Know Our Planet. Ann Arbor, Mich.: Cherry Lake Publishing, 2016.

Levy, Janey. *20 Fun Facts About Machu Picchu.* Fun Fact File: World Wonders! New York: Gareth Stevens Publishing, 2014.

Markovics, Joyce L. *Peru.* Countries We Come From. New York: Bearport Publishing, 2017.

INTERNET SITES

Use FactHound to find Internet sites related to this book.

Visit *www.facthound.com*

Just type 9781515799153 and go.

Check out projects, games and lots more at
www.capstonekids.com

CRITICAL THINKING QUESTIONS

1. What are the three regions of Peru?

2. Why do you think people enjoy traveling to Peru?

3. What are some jobs that Peruvian people have? What might make these jobs hard? What might make them fun?

INDEX